Food Around the World

by Margie Burton, Cathy French, and Tammy Jones

People live all around
the world.

They like to eat many kinds of food.

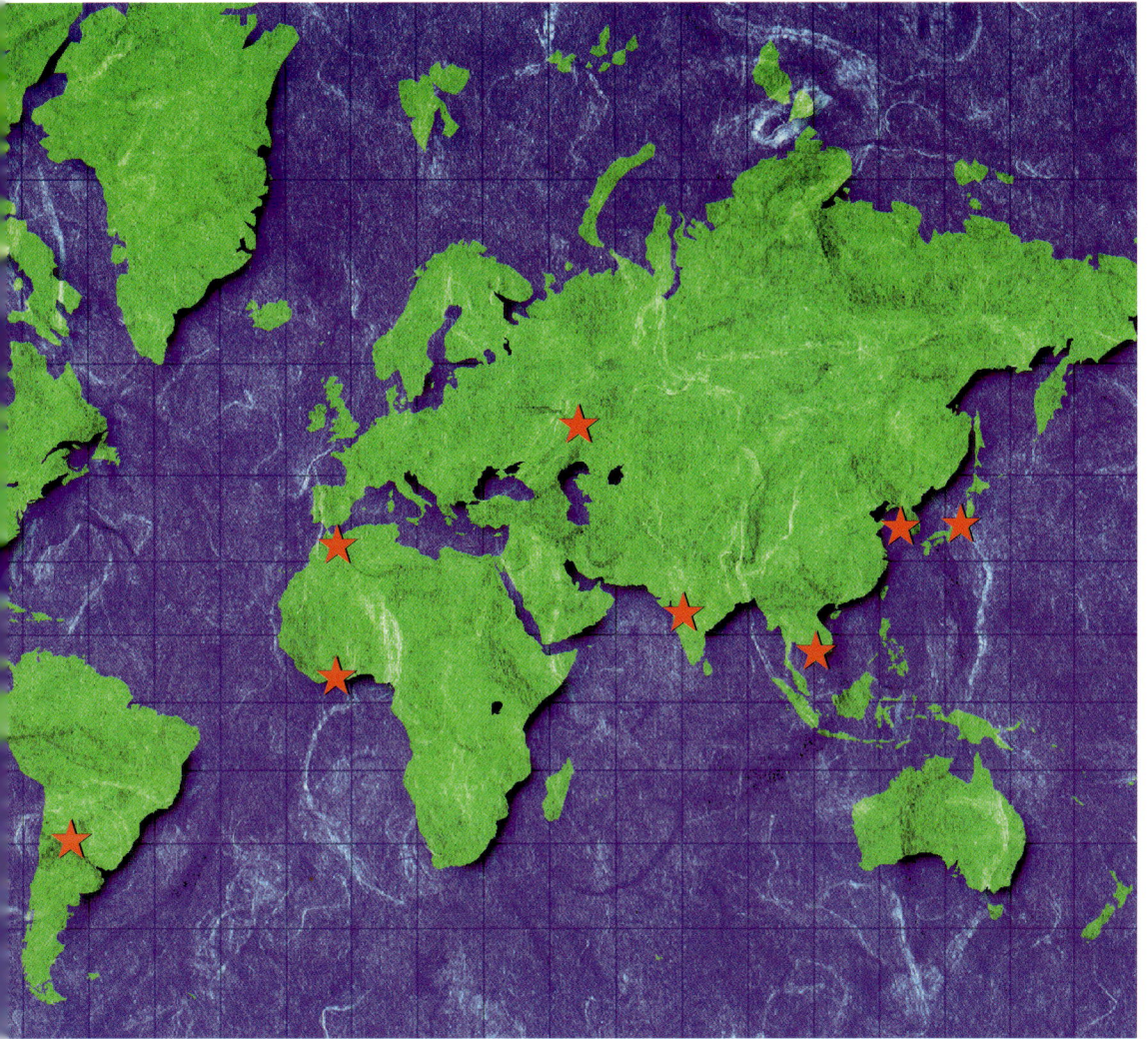

Japan

I like to eat a lot of fish. Sometimes we do not cook the fish. We eat it raw and put it in some seaweed. We eat rice, too.

Do you like to eat vegetables? I do! I eat my vegetables with rice.

Korea

Vietnam

I like to
eat beef
and vegetables
and rice noodles.
I like to put
some lime
on my food.

India

We like to eat fish.
We eat our fish
with rice. We
like to put
a hot, red sauce
on it.

Morocco

I like to eat pasta.
My pasta is so small
that it looks like rice.
I like to eat it with meat.

Do you like my food? It is like bananas. I like to fry them when I eat them.

Ghana

9

Russia

I like to
eat pancakes.
I like to
drink tea, too.

Argentina

I like to
eat meat that
comes from
my ranch. We
have some cows
on our ranch.

Mexico

I like to eat beans.
I eat my beans
in tortillas.
I like to put
hot peppers
into my food.

I like to
eat fish and
some foods
that we hunt
and kill. I
like to hunt
for food
with my dad.

The Arctic

USA

Do you like
to eat my food?
I like to
eat turkey sandwiches.
I make my turkey
sandwiches
at home.

Here is how you can make a turkey sandwich at home:

1. Get the things that you need for your sandwich from the store.

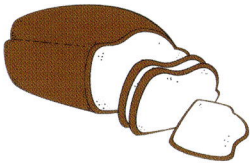

2. First, wash your hands.

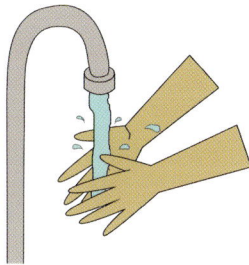

3. Then take two slices of bread and put them on a plate.

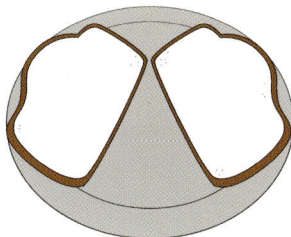

4. Put some turkey on the bread. Then, spread mustard on the turkey.

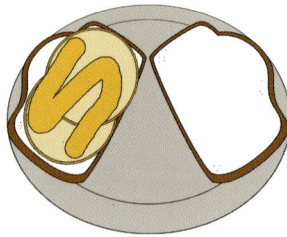

5. Put the lettuce and tomato on the turkey.

6. Finally, put the other slice of bread on top. Eat up!